A Woman's Search For Inner Peace

16 Simple Spiritual Practices
for Everyday Life

Carol Solberg Moss, LCSW
Antoinette Saunders, Ph.D.

"A Woman's Search For Inner Peace," by Carol Solberg Moss LCSW and Antoinette Saunders, Ph.D. ISBN 978-1-60264-720-6.

Published 2011 by Virtualbookworm.com Publishing Inc., P.O. Box 9949, College Station, TX 77842, US. ©2011, Carol Solberg Moss LCSW and Antoinette Saunders, Ph.D. All rights reserved. No part of this publication may be reproduced, stored in a retrieval system, or transmitted in any form or by any means, electronic, mechanical, recording or otherwise, without the prior written permission of Carol Solberg Moss LCSW and Antoinette Saunders, Ph.D.

Manufactured in the United States of America.

Dear Reader,

Thank you for picking up this book. If you are looking for meaning and direction in your life it is our belief that you will find it here.

We wrote this book for women who are starting on their spiritual journey and are looking for guidance and specific tools.

We have tried very hard to keep it simple because the path can seem overwhelming and confusing. We invite you to join Claudia, a middle-aged woman and mother, on a journey with her spiritual psychotherapist, Kathryn. Together they explore 16 different spiritual practices and Claudia discovers how easily all this new information can be integrated into her life, resulting in deeper meaning, contentment and inner peace. Each chapter ends with an exercise that will engage you in a more thoughtful and practical experience of the topic being discussed.

We hope this will make your path easier.

Carol Solberg Moss
Antoinette Saunders
www.awomanssearchforinnerpeacebook.com

To our daughters,
Annie and Emma

We would like to thank Cissi Henrick for her brilliant suggestions, which made the book much better than we ever could have imagined, and Helen Gallagher for her viral guidance, wisdom and support. We are also grateful to Emma Moss for her photography and design talents and Ari Furuya, whose painting graces the cover.

Table of Contents

PART ONE: *STEP ONE*:
BECOMING AWARE
Practice One: Asking for Help   1
Practice Two: Recognizing Victimhood   6
Practice Three: Cultivating Mindfulness   10
Practice Four: Choosing Fear or Faith   18
Practice Five: Thinking Positively   25

PART TWO: *STEP TWO*:
GOING DEEPER
Practice Six: Recognizing Synchronicity   32
Practice Seven: Identifying Your Values   38
Practice Eight: Integrating All Your Parts   48
Practice Nine: Owning Your Life Purpose   56

PART THREE: *STEP THREE*:
PUTTING IT TOGETHER
Practice Ten: Accepting What Is   64
Practice Eleven: Living in Non Judgment   71
Practice Twelve: Letting Go of Outcomes   78
Practice Thirteen: Practicing Forgiveness   84
Practice Fourteen: Living Compassionately   91
Practice Fifteen: Being Grateful   96
Practice Sixteen: Giving Back   102

Bibliography   108
About the Authors   111

Part One: Step One
Becoming Aware

"When dreaming, I'm guided through another
world, time and time again.
At sunrise I fight to stay asleep,
'cause I don't want to leave the comfort of this
place, 'cause there's a hunger, a **longing** to escape,
from the life I live when I'm awake."

Creed

One

"And the day came when the risk to remain tight in the bud was more painful than the risk it took to bloom."

Anais Nin

Looking For Direction And Help

Practice One: Asking for help. When we recognize that we are limited in what we can do for ourselves and others and we find ourselves looking for help, we have crossed the line into the world of belief and spirit. We are surrendering and asking for assistance on a higher plane.

Claudia woke with a start. As her brain slowly kicked into gear, she was met with a familiar dullness in her chest. It wasn't a pain, just a heaviness that had been with her for some time now. She slowly climbed out of bed and walked into the bathroom, purposely not looking at her reflection as she passed by the mirror.

She didn't recognize herself anymore and wondered if others had noticed how much she had changed and that filled her with sadness. Claudia had worked so hard on her home, her kids, her career and her community. She often felt she wasn't good enough, but she had always been able to count on contributing a certain sparkle to any setting. Now that was changing. She felt invisible. As long as she could remember, she believed that if she was good and kind to others and worked hard, she would find happiness. When she did look in the mirror, she realized it wasn't just about the changes she saw. Claudia felt a wave of emotion, as she understood that she was disillusioned and disappointed in herself.

Claudia felt she had little to show for all the years she had spent taking care of her family. Before she met her husband, David, she had been a public relations executive in a large Chicago agency. After their two children, Molly and Jeremy were born, she freelanced until her son was diagnosed with Auditory Processing Disorder at age 7, then quit, wanting to spend more time with him. Last month, David had lost his job. Since then she had gained weight and had trouble sleeping.

As these thoughts swirled in her mind, Claudia sat down on her bed and said out loud, "I don't know what I'm doing. I'm scared. I'm lost." Getting up slowly, Claudia walked back into the bedroom, fighting the urge to crawl back into bed. She picked up the phone sitting on the bedside table and made a call.

"Mom?" she asked. "Are you awake? Can we talk?"

"Hi sweetheart, how are you? You sound tired."

"I'm beyond tired," Claudia replied.

"What do you mean, you are beyond tired?" her mother asked with concern.

"I know this may not make sense," said Claudia, taking a deep breath. "I'm worried about the kids and David, I'm not getting enough sleep, I don't think I'm depressed but I feel anxious all the time." Claudia could feel the familiar sting of tears behind her eyes.

"Oh honey, that sounds awful. How long have you felt this way?" her mother consoled.

"Gosh Mom, that's a great question," Claudia answered as she wiped away a tear. "I don't know. Did you ever feel this way?"

"Yes, after your father and I divorced, I felt lost too."

"So, what did you do?" asked Claudia.

"I focused on being the best mother I could. If it was today, I'm sure I'd get professional help."

"Well, Mom, I never thought I'd hear you say that." After a pause Claudia said, "Let me be honest with you. I feel like I'm spinning my wheels. My marriage is a disappointment, Jeremy is a constant worry and it feels like one of the only light spots in my life has gone underground since Molly left for college."

"Oh sweetie, I'm sorry you're hurting."

"I think I need to talk to someone," Claudia said finally.

"Who?"

"I don't know. And how am I going to pay for it?"

"Let me help you Claudia. It's something I'd like to do."

"Really?" Claudia began to cry. "Thanks Mom. That's so generous of you. So, where do I begin?"

"Where would you like to begin? Can you ask one of your friends? What kind of person would you want to talk to?"

Claudia said, "Someone, I don't know, maybe a woman who has been through this. Hey, I could ask my yoga teacher."

"Really? Your yoga teacher?" her mother responded doubtfully.

"Yes!" Claudia said with new energy that surprised her. "She knows everybody and is so spiritual - I always feel as if she's reading my thoughts before I think them. I'll see her tomorrow at class."

"Sounds like a great idea sweetheart. Let me know how it goes. I know you'll get through this."

Two

"I try to remind myself that we are never promised anything and that what control we can exert is not over the events that befall us but how we address ourselves to them."

Jeanne DuPrau, *The Earth House*

Recognizing Victimhood

> ***Practice Two: Recognizing Victimhood*** *entails accepting that one can only change oneself. Some people stay locked in a victim stance because they, on some level, believe they will lose something by changing. Others may not be aware that they have a choice.*

Claudia got dressed and went to her yoga class. After class she approached her teacher to see if she had a few minutes to talk or perhaps get a quick cup of tea. Lilah said she'd be happy to talk and suggested they go next door to a coffee shop. Claudia noticed that she was a little nervous but excited at the same time. They found an empty table by the window and sat down. Lilah took a small sip of her steaming hot green tea and said, "So, you said you wanted to talk. What's up?"

"I'm stuck," Claudia replied.

"What do you mean, stuck?" Lilah said. "Can you be a little more specific?"

"Yes, today I almost couldn't get up. I vacillate between feeling anxious, angry and deeply tired. I feel responsible for absolutely everything and I resent it. Jeremy, my son, is a real challenge. My husband is preoccupied and doesn't listen to me. I'm tired of complaining to my girlfriends. I feel like such a whiner. See, I'm doing it now. I'm whining and I hate it when my kids whine and ……. the only time my head calms down is when I'm in yoga, but once class is over, my life returns and I'm a mess. I feel lost."

Lilah smiled and said, "You know, this is not an unusual thing for women to go through. I felt that way in my late forties and I thought about having an affair, but knew it would cause more damage than I was prepared to handle. I felt like such a victim in my life and that I had little to no power. I think a lot of women experience this," said Lilah.

"Am I crazy or depressed or what?" asked Claudia.

"I don't think you're crazy and I certainly am not one to make a diagnosis. My sense is that when you're feeling like a victim, you're not in charge of your life."

Claudia felt a wave of emotion pass through her as Lilah spoke.

"What I do know Claudia is that if you continue to see yourself as a victim nothing will change. You will continue to be angry and resentful," said Lilah.

"First off, how can you possibly know me so well? And second, where do I go from here???? How do I balance my life and stop feeling like a victim? How do I put myself in the center of my life when there's no room for me?" Claudia asked.

"There are lots of ways." Lilah continued calmly. "You could talk to a therapist, go to a spiritual director, take classes in meditation, pray, do yoga, read some books, take a walk in nature, start a group, find a mentor, go to a 12-step program - in short, there are many roads you could consider."

"What did you do?" asked Claudia.

"Everyone has their own journey and their own road. In my case, I found Kathryn, a therapist who had a background in spiritual direction," offered Lilah.

"What does spiritual direction mean?" said Claudia.

"Well, she was comfortable in talking about things that went beyond psychotherapy, like connecting us to something larger than ourselves," explained Lilah. "After working with her for a few months I started to feel better, I felt more in control of my life, my inner life anyway."

"Do you mind giving me her name and number?" Claudia asked.

"Of course not, here it is," Lilah said. "And, you might want to think about stepping up your yoga practice as you begin your journey."

Claudia laughed, "I just might want to do that!"

Three

"Wherever you go, there you are."

Jon Kabat-Zinn

Practicing Mindfulness

Practice Three: Cultivating mindfulness involves being fully present in the moment without bias and practicing non-doing. It is a calm awareness of all the senses and emotions, while focusing on the breath.

Claudia went home and called Kathryn and made an appointment for the next day. When she arrived at Kathryn's office, Claudia was struck by how calm she felt when she sat down in a comfortable chair in the waiting room. Looking around she saw pictures of beautiful landscapes and heard the gentle trickle of water in a fountain in the corner. On the table next to where Claudia sat was a bowl of small pebbles, each of which had a word printed on it such as: "Patience," "Serenity" and "Peace." Without having uttered a word yet, Claudia felt she had come to the right place. The door opened and a middle-aged woman with bright blue eyes and soft wavy hair that framed her faced stood smiling at her. Claudia was surprised that she was dressed comfortably and fashionably and she realized that she had been expecting to see something different. She looked like someone Claudia would meet for coffee.

"You must be Claudia," Kathryn smiled. "Welcome! Please come in and make yourself comfortable on my couch."

"OK," replied Claudia as she stood up and walked into the office. Kathryn then asked, "Would you like some tea or a glass of water before you sit down?"

"Um, water would be great, thank you," said Claudia. Kathryn walked over to the bubbler and poured Claudia a glass of water and handed it to her.

"Well, Claudia, how can I help you?" Kathryn asked as she sat down in a chair opposite to her.

"I don't know. I am tired and angry all the time." Claudia took a deep breath. "I am worried about my son, who is 16 and has an Auditory Processing Disorder. My daughter is off at college and I miss her and her absence only highlights my sadness over my marriage which feels stale...and I just feel worn out." Claudia began to cry.

Kathryn handed her a Kleenex.

After a few minutes of silence and when Claudia seemed to be feeling better, Kathryn said, "Claudia, I first want to say, thank you for coming today. I know that it took a lot of courage for you to come here and talk about yourself. I'd like you to know that I really respect you for that."

Claudia was surprised to feel tears forming in her eyes again.

Wiping her eyes, Claudia said, "I'm not sure what just happened there...I guess I'm not used to being acknowledged."

"Can you start again, Claudia and tell me again why you are here?" asked Kathryn.

"I'm anxious and sad and scared and lost all at the same time – a LOT of the time. I wake up with the same feeling every morning, a heavy, hopeless feeling. I want to feel better but I just don't know where to begin. Why is this happening to me? Lilah talked to me about how I'm acting like a victim."

"It makes sense that you might want to blame others for your situation, especially when you feel overwhelmed," said Kathryn. "If we look at that from a spiritual perspective, we can find some opportunities for growth."

"Lilah, my yoga teacher, who used to see you, said that you were a spiritual psychotherapist,"

Claudia said. "I Googled that but I just got more confused."

Kathryn smiled. "I know that the whole world of spirituality and psychotherapy can be confusing. That is why I have defined 16 different practices that can guide you on that journey. In the first few sessions we will focus on your becoming aware of how you think and how that affects how you feel, in the next few sessions we will go deeper into what you believe and how that affects how you behave and finally we will put it all together with the last seven spiritual practices."

"It sounds like you have it all mapped out," Claudia commented.

"Yes," replied Kathryn with a smile. "It can be overwhelming so having a map can be very helpful. And, you have already practiced the first two, which is 'asking for help and recognizing victimhood,'" Kathryn continued.

"So, are you game, Claudia? Are you willing to consider that we are spiritual beings having a human experience?"

"I don't really know what I am signing up for, but I do want help, so yes, let's get started," Claudia answered.

"Let's begin by getting quiet," said Kathryn.

"Don't tell me we're going to pray," said Claudia.

"No – not today anyway," Kathryn smiled. "We just need to calm the waters to see what's going on inside. Now, soften your eyes and focus your attention on the window. What are you aware of?"

Claudia said, "I hear the cars outside and that dog barking."

"Good," said Kathryn. After a few moments she said, "Now, shift your attention to this room. What do you notice?"

"I notice the ticking of the clock, and the smell of your hazelnut coffee," replied Claudia.

After a moment, Kathryn said, "Now, shift your attention inside and hold that focus. What do you notice?" she asked.

"I can feel the air dropping into my lungs, and where my back is a little sore from my yoga class. I can feel my tongue in my mouth and my stomach just growled." Claudia said.

"Now focus on your breathing," Kathryn continued.

Claudia and Kathryn sat in silence for a few more minutes. To mark the end of the silence, Kathryn gently rang a small bell. "What was that like for you Claudia?" she asked.

"I was kind of self-conscious. I had trouble focusing on my breathing. My mind went everywhere. I found myself thinking about what I needed to do when I got home," Claudia said.

"Ah – that would be 'monkey mind' which most people experience, especially in the beginning," Kathryn explained. "The key is to just notice your thoughts, watch them go by like you are watching clouds move across the sky and then return to your breath."

Claudia said. "OK. I'll try that. I will say that I feel more relaxed."

"Great," said Kathryn. "That was your first lesson in Mindfulness – a Buddhist practice that we will be using a lot in our work together. It's not unlike the work you've done in yoga where you have to stay very present in your poses and find a way to breathe. We will be spending much of our time going inward and looking at your internal world – a mysterious journey. How does that sound?"

"I'm a little skeptical, but what do I have to lose? Claudia added.

"Wonderful. I encourage skepticism." Kathryn said. "Another important element of our work is that I'd like to ask that you begin to keep a journal of your thoughts and feelings, as a daily meditation in order to quiet your mind." Kathryn reached into her desk, pulled out a small blank journal and handed it to Claudia. "You can write as much or as little as you'd like. Think that's possible?"

"I'll do my best," said Claudia.

"Thanks for the journal!"

"You're welcome," replied Kathryn. "In addition, I invite you to remember to be mindful when you journal. Try to choose a specific time each day where you go inside and connect to your inner spirit, or sense of something bigger than you – God, Creator, Allah, Source, Light. You may also want to designate a particular corner or area of your house in which to do your daily practice. Some people make an altar that contains meaningful objects or find a favorite chair in which to sit. Can you think of a location in your house where you could make this happen?"

"Yes, I have a window seat in my bedroom that would be perfect. It looks out over my backyard where I'm constantly entertained by nature," Claudia replied.

"Perfect," Kathryn said.

"I'm so glad I came today."

"Me too," Kathryn smiled.

As Claudia walked to her car she noticed that she was more hopeful. She felt that she had a plan, a map, something new to try.

Mindfulness Exercise:

Designate a location in your home for reflection. Include favorite items, i.e. candles, soft pillows, etc.

Commit to a daily practice of journaling in a mindful way. What that looks like is:

1. Engage in your activity by focusing on your breath.

2. Be in total awareness of your internal and external environment.

3. Start writing without any judgment.

Four

"What youth found and must find outside, the man of life's afternoon must find within himself."

Carl Jung

Choosing Fear Or Faith

Practice Four: Choosing between fear or faith involves a leap of – you guessed it – faith. The tasks of the first half of life are external and ego or fear driven, having largely to do with establishing a family and career. The tasks of the second half of life are internal having largely to do with finding meaning in our life and in our death. Negotiating this transition successfully involves faith.

Claudia was not surprised when she found herself looking forward to her next visit with Kathryn. She had been writing in her journal everyday. She had started a list of situations that she wanted help on. Things that she felt she had no control over. She had tried sitting quietly on her own but still found it very challenging. She was curious about learning a new way of thinking. She was not disappointed when Kathryn announced that she wanted to talk to Claudia about fear and faith. After settling down and getting something to drink, Kathryn asked how her week went.

"Nothing has really changed, but I feel more hopeful," Claudia began. "I wrote in my journal and I found that spending time just jotting down my feelings and fears helped me not be so anxious. It was as if by putting them on the paper I no longer had to carry them inside. I also tried sitting still and paying attention to my breath. That was more difficult," she said.

"Claudia, what a great start. I am so pleased that you are writing in your journal. Externalizing your feelings, putting them outside your body does help to calm you down," Kathryn said. "It also gives us a place to start when we are together."

"Before we start on your journal, I wanted to offer you some explanations about what I think you are going through," Kathryn said.

"You mean why I'm so anxious and angry all the time?" Claudia asked.

"Yes," Kathryn replied. "I hope that this whole process will help you understand and change the way you feel."

"The transition between the first and second half of our lives is difficult for most people, and problems often occur during this time," Kathryn said. "Now, most of us don't walk around thinking actively about the meaning of our lives. But it asks an important question. Knowing that we're all aging and headed toward the same ending, how do we want to spend our days: fearful of all the 'What ifs' or trusting that everything will turn out alright? Do we want to walk that path in a state of fear and ego or faith and love?"

"I have thought long and hard about these questions, Claudia," Kathryn said.

"I have come to understand that experiencing life from a perspective of fear or faith is a choice – really a simple choice. I choose faith."

"What do you mean by faith?" asked Claudia.

"A definition from Hebrews in the Bible says, '*Faith is the* substance of things hoped for and the evidence of *things not seen*,'" Kathryn explained.

"I want you to understand that I am not talking about organized religion here, though many find belonging to a Church or Temple or Mosque very comforting," Kathryn said. "I am talking about creating a personal relationship with your God, or Higher Power or The Source. There are many names for that Organizing Force that most of us acknowledge. When we accept the existence of God in our lives we can let go of fear."

"Go on," Claudia interjected.

"Said in a different way, when we are afraid, we cannot experience the comfort and peace that believing in God or something bigger than us can offer us," Kathryn continued. "A favorite 12-step saying is that 'I'd rather live my life as if there is a God and find out there's not, than live my life as if there isn't and find out there is.'"

"I will have to think about this," said Claudia. "I have never heard it put so simply before." After a brief pause, Claudia said, "I guess I do recognize how fear keeps me from feeling peaceful."

"Well, that's a start Claudia," Kathryn said.

"Claudia, you mentioned that you wrote down in your journal a list of the things or events in your life over which you felt that you had no control, is that right?" Kathryn asked.

"Yes I did," replied Claudia.

"What I would like you to do right now is choose one event and describe how it would be different if you believed that everything will be alright, if you trusted that there was a Divine order to things. Let's do it right now. What is the first item on your list?" Kathryn asked.

"My son Jeremy. I am worried that I am not doing enough for him and that I am not a good enough mother," Claudia began.

"OK. Instead of being worried, put faith into the sentence," Kathryn prompted.

After a moment, Claudia said, "How does this sound? I am doing enough for Jeremy because God is in my life and I will get the direction and help I need?"

"How does that feel?" Kathryn asked.

"Amazing. I don't feel so alone and scared."

"Excellent. You are a great student. Now when you have time this week go through your list and change your stories." said Kathryn.

"Remember it's a simple choice. Choosing fear or faith," Kathryn added.

"I will," Claudia said and left with a big smile on her face.

Fear Or Faith Exercise:

This week, make a list of situations or people that you resent or are afraid of. Then add faith in the God of your choice to that scenario and see if it changes anything. If so, how?

_____
_____
_____
_____
_____
_____
_____
_____
_____
_____
_____
_____
_____
_____
_____
_____
_____
_____
_____
_____
_____
_____
_____
_____
_____
_____
_____
_____
_____

Five

"They can because they think they *can*"

Virgil

Thinking Positively

Practice Five: Tapping into the power of positive thinking involves erasing negative thinking and substituting positive self-talk, which is a true form of self-love and nurturance.

Claudia entered Kathryn's office and brushed the mist of rain from her hair.

"Wow, it's really coming down hard out there, isn't it?" Kathryn observed.

"Traffic was a nightmare and I'm such an idiot for forgetting my umbrella," Claudia commented. "But, I'm here now."

"Before we get started on a new practice, tell me Claudia how was your week?" asked Kathryn.

"I really was impressed with the fear or faith choice. I did change my stories like you suggested. One of my fears is that my marriage will never change and that David and I will continue to grow apart. I changed it to choosing to believe that we will get the help we need and that if the marriage ends then that is part of The Bigger Plan too," Claudia said.

"Wow, Claudia, that is amazing," Kathryn commented.

"Thank you and I agree. I am glad that I have written it down because I have to remind myself of that everyday," Claudia said.

Kathryn laughed. "That is why we call them practices because these spiritual principles only work if you keep practicing them. We have another fun exercise to do today. We're going to talk about the negative things you tell yourself, the negative thoughts you – we – all have running through our heads."

"OK," Claudia replied cautiously. "What's the fun part?"

"You'll see," said Kathryn, pulling out a piece of paper. "Now Claudia, have you ever excitedly begun a project, only to find yourself discouraged by it a few hours or days later? Do you ever tell yourself things like, 'I can't do this,' 'I'm not good enough,' and so on?"

"You know I do," Claudia said.

"Let's make a list. This won't be pretty and I don't agree with your judgments, but let's make a list of all the negative things you tell yourself when you get discouraged or that cause you to become discouraged."

After a moment Claudia said, "When I look in the mirror I tell myself I'm fat, when my kids argue I'm sure it's because I'm a bad mom, I know I'm not as accomplished as I'd like to be, I feel old and tired most of the time. Is that what you're looking for?"

"Yes, that's perfect," said Kathryn. "I suspect you've been telling yourself these things for awhile." Claudia nodded. "So these thoughts have created strong neuro-pathways in your brain. It feels very familiar to think these thoughts even though they aren't very affirming, right?"

"Go on," Claudia said.

"We're going to try to form some new neuro-networks by turning these thoughts around. At first they won't feel natural, just like when you start a new exercise program and your body doesn't quite know what it's doing yet, but with time and practice, the new and more positive pathways will be formed," Kathryn explained.

"How will we do that?" asked Claudia.

"I've written these negative thoughts on one side of the page, let's call them tarnished thoughts. On the opposite side of the page, we are going to come up with more positive versions of these thoughts; we'll call them polished thoughts. So, your first tarnished thought was 'I'm fat.' Can you think of a more positive thing to say to yourself about your body?"

"I suppose 'I'm not fat' wouldn't qualify?"

"Nope."

"OK – how about 'I'm healthy.' And for the next one, 'I'm a bad mom,' I could substitute, 'I'm doing my best,' said Claudia. "You know, it feels good to say these positive thoughts. I can feel my chest relaxing."

"Beautiful work, Claudia," Kathryn said, as they continued working on changing her negative thoughts to positive ones. When they'd finished, Kathryn asked Claudia to read her new list out loud every day and to be conscious during the week of the things she said to herself and to substitute positive thoughts for the negative ones.

"Remember to be patient with yourself," Kathryn said. "You've told yourself these messages for a long time, in part to keep yourself safe."

"I thought they were my conscious talking to me," Claudia commented.

"Here's a rule of thumb: if the thought is negative, it's not your conscious, it's just fear," said Kathryn.

"Thanks. Well, it looks like the sun is coming out. I will see you next week," Claudia said.

Claudia stood at the door taking in all the fresh smells released after the spring storm. "I am practicing mindfulness," Claudia said to her self as she walked thoughtfully into the sun. "These practices are powerful. I really can change the way I feel by changing the way I think."

Positive Thoughts Exercise:
1. Take out a piece of paper and fold it in half. On one half make a list of all the negative, or tarnishing thoughts you are aware of that you tell yourself. Make them "I" statements, such as "I am lazy," "I'm not good enough," etc.

2. On the right hand side of the paper, flip the statement over and write the opposite, or as close to opposite as you can make yourself believe. Notice how it feels when you write these statements and how it feels in your body. Be sure that the positive statements do not contain the word, "not," such as "I'm not lazy." A better choice would be "I'm productive."

Example:

NEGATIVE	POSITIVE
I'm lazy	I'm productive
I'm not good enough	I'm good enough
I'm too old	There's still time

Part Two: Step Two:

Digging Deeper

My God, I have no idea where I am going.

I do not see the road ahead of me. I cannot know for certain where it will end.

Nor do I really know myself, and the fact that I think I am following your will does not mean that I am actually doing so.

But I believe that the desire to please you does in fact please you and I hope that I have that desire in all that I am doing.

And I know that if I do this, you will lead me by the right road although I may know nothing about it.

Therefore will I trust you always though I may seem to be lost and in the shadow of death, I will not fear, for you are ever with me and you will never leave me to face my perils alone.

Thomas Merton

Six

"Bidden or not, God is present."

Carl Jung

Recognizing Synchronicity In Your Life

> ***Practice Six:*** *Noticing synchronicity is like discovering magic. Synchronicity is a term first coined by psychologist, Carl Jung, and is the experience of two or more events that are apparently causally unrelated occurring together in a meaningful manner. It can be as subtle as thinking of someone and they phone you or profound as meeting a stranger across a crowded room and knowing you've found your partner.*

Claudia almost skipped into Kathryn's office.

"You seem to be in a good mood today," observed Kathryn.

"I am," Claudia responded as she found her way to her favorite chair and sat down.
"Tell me what is going on," Kathryn said.

"Well, I have been practicing choosing faith over fear and changing my negative thoughts and I make a point of stopping once or twice a day and just noticing where I am. And I am beginning to feel lighter, not so down. But that is not why I am smiling," Claudia said.

Kathryn looked at her expectantly.

"I got this random email advertising a couple's workshop on Love and Respect in a western suburb. It was being sponsored by a Church out there," Claudia began. "I asked David if he wanted to go and he said 'yes.' I almost died. So we went. We spent the day learning more about the difference between men and women and how women value love over respect and men value respect over love. It was fascinating and David and I had some really good discussions," Claudia explained.

"I love how this happens," Kathryn chuckled. "Today we are scheduled to talk about synchronicity and you just told me a story that illustrated it."

Claudia looked confused.

"Do you remember two weeks ago when you were making a list of the things that upset you?"

"Yes," said Claudia, not sure where this was going.

"You were talking about how you were worried about your marriage and you choose to believe that you would get the help you needed. Do you remember?" Kathryn asked.

"Oh yes, I am always worrying about my marriage. No wait I choose faith ..." Claudia said.

"Well, yes," Kathryn laughed.

"Today we are going to talk about synchronicity. Your story about the couple's workshop is an example. Unbidden, seemingly from nowhere you were given the opportunity to get help for your marriage and you acted upon it." Kathryn said.

"Yes. It was strange, in a good way," said Claudia.

"You experienced the mystery of the universe," said Kathryn. "In my belief system nothing happens by accident. When we pay attention, these events happen all the time, reminding us that we are all part of a greater mystery."

"Now, can you think of any other experiences like this where you got help unbidden or someone just said the right answer to a question you were pondering or a song came on the radio that gave an answer to your question?"

Claudia sat back and thought for a moment. "I've noticed that before, but thought it was just coincidence. Now that I think of it, when I asked Lilah for help she gave me your name and you had an opening right away." she said.

"What if it's not coincidence?" queried Kathryn. "Be observant this week, write in your journal and see what happens when you ask for help."

Recognizing Synchronicity Exercise:
1. Think back over your week and identify any experiences that you had labeled coincidence. Choose one and write about it in detail.

2. Consciously ask for help this week and notice how it shows up. Record it here or in your journal.

Seven

Just as your car runs more smoothly and requires less energy to go faster and farther when the wheels are in perfect alignment, you perform better when your thoughts, feelings, emotions, goals, and values are in balance.

Brian Tracy

Identifying Your Values

> *Practice Seven: Personal values are the things that define who you are,* what excites you and what you stand for. Values aren't morals. *They are principles that give our lives meaning and they change throughout one's lifespan. Our actions reflect our values.*

As they both settled into their chairs, Kathryn looked at Claudia, who was looking through her journal.

"Claudia, it looks like you have been doing a lot of writing," observed Kathryn.

"I have. This week was a really interesting one. I have been really enjoying looking at my life in a different way," Claudia said.

"Tell me what you mean."

"Well last week we talked about the fact that there were no coincidences. I wanted to see if I agreed, so I started to really pay attention to all the subtle things that happened around me," Claudia said.

"Can you give me an example?" asked Kathryn.

"Yes. I was in my office at home, worrying about Jeremy... and NPR had a guest lecturer who was an expert on teenagers who had Auditory Processing problems. I felt like he was talking to me. I wrote down all his advice and I ran out and got his book. I am a believer now. That was unreal," Claudia said.

"It does seem unreal but it's not," Kathryn said.

"I know...."

"What's on the schedule today, Kathryn? I am really enjoying this process and I feel better. My mother noticed that I look happier and that I am not so prickly," Claudia said.

"I am so pleased to hear that Claudia.
Well, today we are going to talk about values that give our lives meaning."

"What do you mean?"

"We all have values - they aren't the same as morals, they aren't right or wrong. They are what give our life meaning and give us a reason for getting up the morning. Our actions reflect our values," Kathryn explained.

"Can you give me an example of what you mean?" asked Claudia.

"When my children went off to college, I realized I still needed another way to honor my value of nurturing, so I began to tutor."

"I think I know what my values are, be a good mother, a good wife. ..." Claudia began.

"It's not quite that easy." Kathryn chuckled. "We will figure out together what makes you tick. I'm wondering which values are truly yours as opposed to the ones into which you were born, such as your religion, your socioeconomic situation and so on. Have you been having any physical symptoms such as headaches, trouble sleeping, eating too much or not enough?"

"I'm not as rested as I'd like to be and I admit I crave sweets," said Claudia. "Why?"

"Well, when we're not honoring our values and our truth, our bodies talk to us in the form of symptoms and tell us that things are out of sync," answered Kathryn.

"I thought I was just being lazy and needed to go to Weight Watchers -- again," sighed Claudia.

Kathryn smiled and said, "Claudia, can you take out your journal?"

"Yes, I've got it right here," said Claudia.

"I'd like you to write about a peak experience in your life. Something you did that stands out, an experience that was really important to you," said Kathryn. "It could have happened recently or a long time ago, the timing doesn't matter as much as the impact it had on you."

After thinking for a few minutes, she began to write. When she finished she looked up.

"Can you read me what you wrote Claudia?"

Claudia started to read, "One memory that stands out is when our family went kayaking last summer down the Platte River in Northern Michigan. The day was warm, the sky was gorgeous and the water was clear and also quite warm. We had two kayaks for the four of us and we just had so much fun paddling down the river. We sang songs and joked and everyone got along. The best part was at the end, the river emptied into Lake Michigan in a fairly dramatic way. On the bottom of the river were beautiful stones that you could see and when it met the lake, there was a rush of the

41

waters meeting each other. When you looked up you could see the Sleeping Bear Dunes and it seemed as if we were somewhere very exotic and nature had provided a beautiful surprise for us."

Kathryn said, "What a wonderful family memory. I can see why you chose to tell me about it. While you were talking I wrote down the values I heard you articulate. This list is not complete, only a beginning and they are in no particular order, but they were all present in this experience."

"What did you hear?" asked Claudia with curiosity.

"I heard that you value nature, your family, the sky, connections, harmony, fun, movement and adventure," Kathryn began. "Is this resonating with you?"

"Yeah," said Claudia. "Keep going."

With excitement, they continued their conversation.

"Which of these values, Claudia, do you want to have more present in your life?" asked Kathryn.

"Having fun with my family. Doing things together in nature," Claudia responded.

"Do you have any ideas about how you could do that? " Kathryn wondered.

"Well, we could make a point of the three of us walking the dog together after dinner," Claudia said. "You know, I get in my mind that things won't change but I am beginning to see that I may be the problem," said Claudia.

"I don't know if you are the problem, Claudia. But I know that the people around you will change in response to you, if you change," Kathryn said.

"I certainly have a lot to think about. Thank you so much Kathryn," Claudia said as she stuffed her journal back into her bag.

"I will look forward to seeing you next week Claudia," Kathryn called as Claudia left.

Values Exercise:

Write about your own peak experience. Notice how you feel as you write. Using the Values worksheet, review your story and begin to list what values show up. You will end up with ten to twenty words. After you have your list:

1. Prioritize them

2. Review them and rate them on a scale of 0-10 (0=not at all and 10=couldn't be better) as to how fully you are living in that value.

3. Choose two values to focus on.

4. Identify two actions you could do to raise the rating.

5. Commit to an action and do it.

LIST OF VALUES WORKSHEET

ACHIEVEMENT	LOYALTY
ACKNOWLEDGEMENT	OPENNESS
ADVENTURE/EXCITEMENT	PERSONAL GROWTH/EDUCATION
AESTHETICS/BEAUTY	MASTERY/EXCELLENCE
ALTRUISM	MUSIC
AUTONOMY	NATURE
CLARITY	ORDERLINESS
COMMITMENT	PARTNERSHIP
CONNECTING	POWER
CREATIVITY	PRIVACY/SOLITUDE
EMOTIONAL HEALTH	PROFESSIONALISM
ENVIRONMENT	RECOGNITION
FAMILY	RESPECT
FREEDOM	SAFETY
FUN	SECURITY
HONESTY	SELF-CARE
HUMOR	SPIRITUALITY
JOY	TRUST
LEADERSHIP	VITALITY
LOVE	

Eight

"Where you stumble, there your treasure lies."

Joseph Campbell

Integrating All Your Parts

> *Practice Eight: The "shadow" is an unclaimed part of oneself that can be the source of rich information and personal growth. Acknowledging our shadow helps us to become whole.*

Claudia walked stiffly into Kathryn's office. She nodded to Kathryn and sat down with a thud.

"Claudia, what's going on? You look very unhappy," Kathryn said.

"Actually, I am furious. I am trying hard to contain my anger but it is not working," Claudia fumed.

Kathryn waited patiently as Claudia told her story.

"Last night Jeremy got arrested. I am so angry I can't see straight," Claudia said as she reached for a Kleenex. "I alternate between being angry and scared. Jeremy pushes all my buttons. He has since he was little." Claudia started to cry.

After a few minutes Kathryn asked Claudia to tell her what happened.

Claudia took a deep breath and said, "The kids have today off for a teacher in-service. Last night, Jeremy asked if he could take the car and visit his friend Mike. He said his homework was under control so we said 'yes,' but to be home by 11. At 11:45 he called us from the police station saying that he had been arrested for violating curfew...and worse, he argued with the arresting officer so he's been charged with resisting arrest."

There was more silence while Claudia collected her thoughts.

"I went to the police station with David. The minute I saw Jeremy I let him have it. I couldn't help myself I was so angry. The policeman asked me to go into a separate room and calm down," Claudia said between tears.

"I am so ashamed of my anger. And I'm so terrified of losing him." she sobbed. "I'm embarrassed to say this, but the only time I feel powerful is when I'm yelling at my kids or husband and I know I should find a different way to do things and then I feel so guilty about it that I feel paralyzed and very, very small."

"If my child was arrested and argued with the police I'd feel exactly the same way," Kathryn said.

"Really?" Claudia asked, and then blew her nose. "Thank you for understanding how I feel."

"You said that you felt very small... as in young?" Kathryn asked.

"I guess," replied Claudia.

"And... I notice that you're equating power with anger?" Kathryn observed.

"I never thought of it that way," reflected Claudia, "but I suppose I do feel powerful when I'm angry, but I'm so ashamed of my anger."

"Well, it's interesting to me that you're ashamed of your anger. In psychology we would call that your shadow, a part of yourself that you're not comfortable with. Claudia, I know that you are worried about Jeremy and I would be happy to talk to you about helping him, but right now can we focus on you?" Kathryn asked.

"Yes, I need all the help that I can get right now," Claudia said with a sigh.

"Let's talk about ways you can use your anger to work for you. Let's go back to that shadow," Kathryn suggested.

"OK," Claudia said.

Kathryn began, "I have an exercise that I find really helpful. Think about Jeremy right now. What is it about him that drives you nuts? Describe a situation."

"Jeremy is just so passive, arrogant and uncooperative. He promises to do things and he doesn't do them. Actually he lies. He says to us that he has done his homework and he hasn't. It's his dishonesty that really bothers me. I just can't trust him." Claudia said, shaking her head. "I get so angry."

"What is the unclaimed part of you?" Kathryn asked.

"I don't understand," Claudia said. "I'm telling you about him. He is so passive and dishonest and so manipulative."

Kathryn said, "Bear with me - now I want you to take that anger and notice where you feel it in your body."

Claudia took a breath and after a moment said, "My stomach is killing me."

"Now close your eyes and focus on that sensation. What is it trying to tell you?"

Claudia sat in silence for some time. Then she said, "Pay attention to me. I have something to say."

"What is it saying?"

"Hmm," Claudia paused. Then with purpose she said, "It's telling me that there are things I need to say and I haven't been speaking up. I have felt taken advantage of and have been guilty of complaining too much without taking action to change the situation." Claudia took a deep breath and unprompted said, "Wow, my stomach is starting to feel better."

"How can you bring that into your everyday life?" Kathryn asked.

"I could sit quietly more often," Claudia replied. "And realize that when I have a lot of emotion or tension that my body is trying to tell me something. I can see how paying attention to my body and giving it a voice helps me feel more connected to myself."

"OK. Now with that insight how do you want to react with Jeremy?" asked Kathryn.

"Well, first of all I don't want to be so reactive. I have been practicing sitting still, being more present, I know how much I value my family, I know how to choose faith not fear, I know how to be positive," Claudia reflected.

After a few minutes of sitting still, Claudia said, "What I want to say to Jeremy is .. 'Jeremy, I am very disappointed in you, but I believe in you and I am looking forward to hearing how you are going to fix this.' I am going to say it calmly and with love."

"How does your stomach feel?"

"Much better. Thank you. That was very helpful and I don't feel so powerless now," Claudia noticed.

"Claudia, I suggest that you write all this down in your journal so you can refer to it," Kathryn said.

As Claudia turned on the car she paused, she took a deep breath and realized she'd taken another big step in her journey.

Integration Exercise:

1. Name one or two people who drive you crazy and list the characteristics that you can't stand.

2. Choose one that has the most energy and, taking a deep breath, ask yourself what part of that characteristic is yours that you can't own.

3. Hold this discovery gently and with no judgment.

4. Decide how you can bring this new knowledge into your life. Is there an action you need to take or is it simply to acknowledge? For example, if the unclaimed part is anger, how can you constructively bring anger into your life?

_____
_____
_____
_____
_____
_____
_____
_____
_____
_____
_____
_____
_____

Nine

> "Nothing contributes so much to tranquilize the mind as a steady purpose – a point on which the soul may fix its intellectual eye."
>
> *Mary Wollstonecraft Shelley*

Owning Your Life Purpose

Practice Nine: Life purpose is not one's job or vocation. It is the reason we exist here on earth. Our purpose is to bathe all our actions in love.

Claudia plopped down in her chair and looked much better than she had the session before.

"How are you doing, Claudia?" asked Kathryn. "How did things go with Jeremy after you left here?"

Claudia sighed, "Better, not great, but better."

"Tell me a little more," Kathryn prompted.
"Well, when I got home, Jeremy was there, as you know he had the day off. David and I had

decided the night before that Jeremy would be grounded indefinitely until we could come up with a plan," Claudia began.

Kathryn nodded.

"So I suggested to David that we ask Jeremy to come up with a plan that would help us trust him again. Jeremy is still thinking about it. He has changed a little in that he doesn't seem so passive. But I'm not sure he's sorry. This morning he said in passing that he had made an appointment with the school counselor," Claudia said.

"Very interesting isn't it? Instead of reacting to Jeremy you put the ball in his court," Kathryn observed. "How do you feel?"

"I am still trying to take it in. I am not so angry. But the remaining anger has helped me stay clear about what I expect from him. I feel more in control. And more loving towards him," said Claudia.

"Good job Claudia," said Kathryn.

"I know. Thank you Kathryn."

"Are you ready for the next practice?"

"Absolutely, you have my full attention."

"Have you ever thought about why you are here and what your purpose is? What do you know for sure about your existence?" asked Kathryn.

"My purpose is to take care of my husband and kids, clean the house, make dinner, and exercise so I can still fit in my jeans," Claudia joked.

"Those are tasks or jobs, but that's not your life's purpose," smiled Kathryn. "What's underneath all those? What motivates those actions?"

"Duty? Responsibility?" replied Claudia.

"Just for the sake of this conversation, what if your purpose was simply to love? To choose love in all your actions? What if love is all that matters? The Dalai Llama says we're put on earth to experience joy and spread it."

"Sounds good, but how do I do it?" said Claudia.

"To borrow from 12-step thinking, it would be to simply do the next most loving thing, whatever or wherever you find yourself. I suspect you're already living a version of your life purpose but just not as consciously as you'd like. It's not some big discovery that's outside of your world, you just haven't acknowledged or named it as your purpose. But, if you are in motion and adding value, you are achieving it."

"I'm with you," said Claudia.

"The challenge, for all of us, is how we express that love in action in our lives. For some, that love is expressed through mothering, for others, through communication, or healing, or the creative arts."

Kathryn pulled out a worksheet and handed it to Claudia. "There are two questions here I'd like you to answer. Your answers will help us get some clarity on your life purpose," Kathryn explained. "Take your time." She handed the sheet and a pen to Claudia and took a sip of her coffee. On the sheet were the following questions:

What are you passionate about?

What brings tears of joy?

After some time when Claudia had finished writing, Kathryn said, "As you read through your answers, did anything surprise you? Did any themes emerge?"

Claudia reviewed her sheet, "Hmmm - well, I did notice that I started to tear up when I wrote about my family, my children and my husband. I also wrote about how much I loved being in PR. I felt so useful, so alive and connected."

"So.... what might your life be like if you were working in PR right now?" Kathryn asked.

"I would be very busy but fulfilled. I stopped working so I could focus on Jeremy and his learning problems. I could go back to work, maybe part-time. I would like to focus on something that adds value to the world, something with heart and environmental integrity, not a product with a big company," said Claudia.

"What would you like to work with?"

"I don't know - maybe something to do with learning disabilities, something to do with kids for sure," Claudia said.

"Sounds like a direction. I am looking forward to hearing where you take this," Kathryn said.

"Me too. See you next week," said Claudia as she dug her keys out of her bag.

Life Purpose Exercise:

Answer the following questions:

1. What are you passionate about?
_____
_____
_____
_____
_____
_____

2. What brings you tears of joy? Keep writing until you are crying tears of joy.
_____
_____
_____
_____
_____
_____
_____
_____
_____
_____
_____
_____
_____
_____
_____
_____
_____

Part Three: Step Three

Spiritual Practices In Action

I thank you God for most this amazing day;
for the leaping greenly spirits of trees and a blue
true dream of sky;
and for everything which is natural which is
infinite which is
yes.

e.e. cummings

Ten

"For after all, the best thing one can do when it is raining is to let it rain."

Henry Wadsworth Longfellow

Accepting What Is

Practice Ten: Accepting "What Is," as opposed to what we want, involves the willingness to experience ourselves and our life exactly as it is. We enjoy genuine freedom when we let go of the struggle of control and relax into the moment.

After settling in to their chairs, Kathryn said, "How are you Claudia? How is Jeremy doing? Any thoughts about your life's purpose?"

"Funny you should ask, because all those answers are tied together. Jeremy is doing better, much better. He asked David and me to come in and talk to the school counselor. We did. The whole meeting was about how we don't listen to him. That we expect him to mess up, so he has given up on trying to please us," Claudia explained.

"This is important," Kathryn offered.

"Yes, well the counselor was telling us that they are trying to launch a parent/student communication workshop. And I offered to help with the promotion, the PR," Claudia said.

"Oh, that's perfect Claudia," said Kathryn.

"I know, it also smacks of synchronicity don't you think?" Claudia asked.

"It sure does. Oh, I am so pleased for you Claudia," said Kathryn.

"So how is your relationship with Jeremy going?"

"He said to me just yesterday, 'Hey Mom we are on the same team now.' I was so moved I gave him a big hug. Everyone seems so much more relaxed. David even seems happier," Claudia said.

"OK," Kathryn said, "This might be a challenge since everything seems to be going well in your life right now but today the practice is 'accepting what is.'"

"What I would like you to do right now is to think about something in your life that you feel powerless over and you are resenting it, resisting it," Kathryn said.

"It is true that things are going better, but I am facing something with David that I am not happy about," Claudia said.

"What is that?" Kathryn asked.

"As you know David is out of work and I have a lot of trouble accepting the way he is looking for a job. He's all over the map and it seems to me is wasting a lot of time either talking to people who can't help him or surfing the internet."

"I can understand why you'd be upset. So, I'm asking you to look at your situation differently," Kathryn said gently. "I'm asking you to consider that there may be another way of looking at it that can change the way you feel."

"OK," Claudia said hesitantly.

"Just sit there for a minute and instead of pushing against this information just sit mindfully and in acceptance. Close your eyes, and take in the reality that David is looking for work in his own way. Feel your breath drop into your body. Keep breathing. Breathe into the acceptance of things the way they are right this very minute. What do you notice?

Claudia sat with her eyes shut for a long time. Finally she said, "I notice that my heart isn't beating so fast -- I feel calmer and more relaxed. But he still doesn't have a job."

"Can you just accept that?"

"I'm willing to keep working on it," Claudia said.

"Excellent," said Kathryn softly.

Accepting "What Is" Exercise:

Recognize that when we resist change we are probably being fearful. For a day, practice total acceptance.

Step 1: Recognize and name the event. For example: I recognize and accept that my child just spilled his milk.

Step 2: Set an affirmation. For example: I accept that I can't control that the milk spilled.

Step 3: Observe the information without any judgment – just notice it.

Step 4: Using your breath, breathe in the situation and on your exhale, release the situation and bless it by putting a light around it or whatever ritual feels right to you.

Step 5: Use this space to write your examples of "accepting what is."

Eleven

Those who love you are not fooled by mistakes you have made or dark images you hold about yourself. They remember your beauty when you feel ugly; your wholeness when you are broken; your innocence when you feel guilty; and your purpose when you are confused.

African saying

Practicing Non-Judgment

> *Practice Eleven: Non-judgment is a challenging practice that invites a neutral stance in any experience, allowing one to observe without getting caught in the rightness or wrongness of a situation.*

As they sat down Kathryn asked Claudia, "How did your week of practicing 'Accepting What Is' go?"

"You know it is interesting. When I accept that I can't change the situation, I am calmer and everything around me seems lighter. The situation doesn't change but somehow it becomes less important," Claudia reported.

"Are you referring to David and his job search?"

"Yes, that and some other things. Mostly around Jeremy and David. I can't change them, so accepting the way they are really helps me. I am not so angry and frustrated," Claudia said.

"Well, you are going to like today's practice," Kathryn offered. "It is similar in some ways to 'Accepting What Is.'"

"What is the practice?"

"Practicing Non-Judgment," Kathryn said.

"Non-Judgment does sound spiritual and hard to do," Claudia commented. "For me, anyway."

"You know Claudia since we have been together I have noticed how hard you are on yourself," Kathryn said.

"I do have high expectations of myself and others," Claudia said seriously.

"How does that make you feel when you or others don't live up to your expectations?"

"Resentful," Claudia began. "Angry. Disappointed. And angry -- did I say angry?"
"Why does it make you angry?" Kathryn asked.

"There is a right and wrong way to do everything. And usually people or I do it wrong." Claudia replied quickly.

"Let me tell you a story that I've found helpful," Kathryn said. "Once there was a smart woman who used to live her life as if she were climbing up a narrow mountain trail in order to find peace and deep satisfaction, thinking that if she did everything the right way she would reach her goal of satisfaction and nirvana. Behind her were slower climbers who she judged as slackers and in front of her were climbers who she judged herself against and always found herself lacking. She came to a clearing where all the climbers were joined together around a warm fire. They all shared their stories of bravery and defeat and she realized they were all on the same journey and had arrived at the same time. Do you have a sense as to what this story is about?"

"Yea - it's pretty lonely being on a narrow path," Claudia responded.

"Yes, and in this world of spirit there is no hierarchy - no one is judged for being faster or slower - we're all joined together in a circle of pain and joy. We're all the same. So, how would your days be different if you were to choose to live around the warm campfire?" asked Kathryn.

"Wow - let me think about that," Claudia said. "I guess I would stop judging myself and get off the narrow path."

"If you remove judgment, what would you put in its place?" Kathryn asked.

After a long pause, Claudia said softly, "I don't know."

"How about compassion and love?" Kathryn asked gently.

"That would feel wonderful," Claudia said.

"It does feel good. Claudia, I would like you to think of a situation that has happened recently where you judged your self harshly," said Kathryn.

"That's not hard to do. I am always coming up short."

"Well, give me an example."

"Ok... Just this morning, we got a call from Molly who's away at college. She was upset because she was sure she did poorly on her math test. I was rushing around trying to get Jeremy off to school and I snapped at her. 'I don't have time for this now Molly, you should have studied harder and only have yourself to blame.' She hung up on me. Of course I called her back and apologized. But I have felt bad about it all morning."

"That is a good example. What would happen if instead of judging yourself you substituted compassion and love?" asked Kathryn.

"I wouldn't be riddled with guilt. I would be less anxious, easier to be around. And I would have compassion for the stress that Molly is feeling."

"Now you can add 'Non-Judgment' to your spiritual practice tool box," Kathryn smiled.

Practicing Non-Judgment Exercise:

Make a list of situations where you judge yourself or others as lacking.

Choose the one that is most difficult and write about that situation with love and compassion instead of judgment.

Twelve

"I try to remind myself that we are never promised anything, and that what control we can exert is not over the events that befall us but how we address ourselves to them."

Jeanne DuPrau

Letting Go Of Outcomes

*Practice Twelve: **Letting go of our attachment to outcomes** is a spiritual challenge of doing our best in the moment and surrendering the outcome to God.*

Claudia walked into Kathryn's office fighting back tears. After a few moments, she said, "Well, I guess my little girl isn't so little anymore."

"What happened? Is she OK?" Kathryn asked.

"Take a look at this, "Claudia said, holding a picture on her phone up to Kathryn. "What is it?" Kathryn asked. "It's Molly's new look. She had the septum of her nose pierced and instead of talking it over with me, she just did it and then sent me the picture with a caption saying, 'check this out.'"

"She's definitely becoming her own person, isn't she? If she had called you, what would you have said?" asked Kathryn.

"I don't have a problem with pierced ears, and I remember when I took her to have hers done, but I would have pointed out the health hazards of nose piercing, as well as my personal opinion, which as I think of it, is pretty judgmental," said Claudia. "I did call her and told her I was surprised and disappointed. She said that she just won't tell me about the next time she does it."

Kathryn paused and quietly said, "Claudia? What are you afraid of?"

Claudia took a breath and sat back. "I'm afraid she's going to hurt herself and I won't be there to comfort her. There's something about your child piercing their skin that is really upsetting. I keep seeing her beautiful flawless skin as a baby and I just hurt all over."

"Really, Claudia, how much control do you have in the long run?" Kathryn asked. "At some point you have to let go of the outcome and trust in her and know that she's a smart girl and can take care of herself."

"How do I let go here? I love her so much and right now, am disappointed too," Claudia asked anxiously.

"Of course you love her. And yet, we're so limited in our ability to control the outcome of most situations. All we can really control is how we show up, our intention and what we put into it. If we've done our job thoroughly, then we can walk away with the feeling of a job well done and have faith that the outcome will be for the best, even when our kids do things we don't like."

Claudia sighed as Kathryn spoke.

"In a spiritual practice, it's letting go and letting God. It's a choice between living in fear and the illusion of control or living in faith by doing the best we can," Kathryn said. "Let me share with you the Serenity Prayer, which is used in 12-step programs. It is a wonderful tool for clarifying what we can and cannot change. It is:

God, grant me the serenity to accept the things I cannot change, the courage to change the things I can, and the wisdom to know the difference.

"The only thing you can really change around Molly's piercing is the way you see it," Kathryn said. "If we think of the prayer as a filter, you're asking God to help you accept things you can't change, which in this case is a piercing and the courage to change the things you can, which in this case is your reaction. The final line speaks to discernment and often, when we're upset, it's hard to know what you can change and cannot."

Claudia leaned forward and said, "I don't want to this get in the way of my relationship with my daughter."

"It won't, I can see that already," Kathryn replied.

After a pause Claudia said, "You know, Kathryn, 'Accepting What Is,' 'Living in Non-Judgment,' and 'Letting Go of the Outcome' all have a similar feel to them."

"They do. As spiritual practices they all are founded on trust and love." Kathryn agreed.

"It is so simple and yet so complex," said Claudia.

"Yes, that is true. Next session we will talk about Forgiveness, the foundation of all spiritual practices. Have a great week Claudia and keep up the good work."

"I will because these practices work," Claudia said. "I'm feeling better about the piercing."

Kathryn gave Claudia a warm hug and she was out the door.

Letting Go Of Outcomes Exercise:

Make a list of all the situations over which you feel powerless.

Using the Serenity Prayer as a filter, review the situations and identify where you are able to take action and where you truly are able to let go.

Thirteen

"When a deep injury is done us, we never recover until we forgive."

Alan Paton

Practicing Forgiveness

> *Practice Thirteen: Practicing forgiveness* entails a conscious and deliberate ongoing act of letting go of resentment, anger or indignation over real or perceived offenses that we carry. Self-forgiveness involves letting go of the unforgiving standards of perfection that we heap upon ourselves. Forgiving others is letting go of the unforgiving standards of perfection that we heap on others.

Kathryn took off her glasses, looked at Claudia and said, "Do you remember that we agreed to talk about Forgiveness today."

"Yes, I remember," said Claudia.

"I wanted to respond to the phone call you made during the week and tell you again how sorry I am that you had to put your dog down. Losing a pet is exquisitely painful."

"Thanks for understanding," Claudia said softly.

"I also wanted to talk about how hurt you were by your husband's reaction to the death of your dog, Daisy, and the lack of support you felt from him. Where are you with that today?" asked Kathryn.

"Well," Claudia said, "I'm still really angry, hurt, disappointed and confused by how he could be so nonchalant about an animal that had been part of our life for 15 years. I tried practicing Non-Judgment and that worked for a few minutes and then I just got angry again. I was able to accept Daisy's death and not blame myself for not doing more for her. But David's lack of concern really upset me."

"I can see why you would be disappointed and upset. So, let's talk about Forgiveness."

"Why should I forgive him?" said Claudia adamantly. "He let me down, I'm not ready to forgive him and if I do I'm saying that his behavior was OK. That's crazy in my book."

"We forgive for ourselves so we're not so caught up in our anger," replied Kathryn. "There's a saying that when we don't forgive, it's like taking poison and waiting for the other person to die. All that negativity is toxic to our system."

"But he really hurt me," Claudia emphasized.

"Yes, that's clear." Kathryn agreed. "But do you want to stay in that feeling of hurt?"

"For now, yes," said Claudia. After a pause she said, "but probably not forever."

"What I'm saying is that practicing forgiveness is letting go of your negative feelings by choosing to step back from the situation, not stay in the poison of resentment," explained Kathryn. "Forgiveness is a spiritual practice. It is an ongoing process, not a one-shot deal. Every time you think of Daisy and how David wasn't there for you, it's an opportunity to take care of the hurting part of yourself."

Claudia took a deep breath.

"Claudia, right now I would like you to rewrite the story of David and Daisy and instead of being angry write the story as if you forgave him. Make sure that you include how forgiving him has made you feel," Kathryn suggested.

After a few minutes of writing, Claudia looked up and said, "By substituting forgiveness instead of anger and resentment in my story, I felt a kind of love. Dare I say it feels almost like a miracle?"

"You know Claudia, the human response would be to be angry at David for his insensitivity. But the spiritual choice is to forgive," said Kathryn.

"Yes, I see what you mean. I also understand that forgiving is a practice that you choose to do over and over again until the anger and resentment are no longer there," Claudia said.
"That's why we call these practices..." Kathryn began.

"I know, because we have to practice them over and over again," Claudia said, finishing Kathryn's sentence.

"You are a great student Claudia."

Forgiveness Exercise:

Forgiving others:
Write about a current situation where you feel wronged by someone and then rewrite the situation as if you've stepped back and forgiven the person. Pay attention to what you notice.

Forgiving self:
Forgiving oneself is just as important, if not more so, than forgiving others. There is great peace and serenity that come with self acceptance.

Make a list of things you need to forgive yourself for. For example: harsh words, telling white lies, etc. Be honest here. Use this space to reflect on these and how often the opportunity arises for you to forgive yourself.

Fourteen

"Rejoice with those who rejoice; mourn with those who mourn."

Romans 12:15

Living Compassionately

Practice Fourteen: Compassion means, "to suffer together." It is thought to be a deeper form of empathy. Eckhart Tolle said, "It is the awareness of a deep bond between yourself and all creation."

Claudia sat down and sighed.

Kathryn said, "Wow, that was a big sigh."

"Well," Claudia began, "I'm feeling kind of heavy-hearted today."

Claudia, before we get started can you tell me how the forgiveness practice went?" asked Kathryn.

"Actually, it all ended well. We had a funeral for Daisy in our backyard. Even Molly joined us on speaker phone. We each told our favorite stories about Daisy. David was participating but not really engaged. I decided to let it go, to forgive him. My anger wasn't serving any purpose and it was just making me feel worse," said Claudia.

"Yes, Claudia, forgiving is a way of letting go. And we do it for ourselves. It's a choice, a spiritual choice," Kathryn said.

"Later, I found out that he's really overwhelmed and concerned about his widowed mother, whose breast cancer has returned. He found out about it the day Daisy died, but hadn't told me. I feel so conflicted – sad for her and angry at him for not telling me so I could have sympathized and not judged him so harshly," Claudia said.

"I'm so sorry to hear that. What awful news and it makes sense that he wasn't as sensitive to you as you would have liked. Thank you for filling me in."

"It's even more complicated since she and I don't really get along. I've tried to have a relationship with her over the years but it just hasn't worked and now I'm not sure what the implications are for this diagnosis." Claudia explained.

"Implications? What do you mean?" Kathryn asked.

"Might she have to live with us? Can she afford treatment? What if she dies? David can hardly speak about it and I feel shut out and then that makes me angry. We're going to see her this weekend and I'm not in a good place. In fact, I'm kind of dreading it." Claudia said.

Kathryn paused and then said, "Those are all valid questions and concerns. Claudia, do think that there might be some shadow issues here?"

"I don't know...."

"I have a challenge for you," Kathryn said.

"What?"

"Try holding them with compassion this weekend," Kathryn offered.

"How do I do that?" asked Claudia.

"Try accepting and holding them without judgment and surround them with love. Try that right now, Claudia. Close your eyes and see David and your mother-in-law. Without judgment, look at them with new eyes. Look at them with kindness, empathy, benevolence, concern and care."

"Oh, my -- that changes everything doesn't it?" Claudia said. "When I picture them right now, I see them as vulnerable and scared, not unlike me."

"Interesting insight Claudia," Kathryn paused for a moment.

"How do you feel about the weekend now?" Kathryn asked.

"I feel more grounded and closer to the person I aspire to be," Claudia replied. "I'll tell you how it goes."

Compassion Exercise:

Breath Of Love

1. Close your eyes and think about the parts of self that need some love and compassion (example: your weight, your impatience with your children or husband, your jealousy of your neighbor, or gossiping about a friend). Breathe love into these parts of yourself.

2. Bring to mind problematic people in your life. Breathe love onto these people.

3. Bring to mind problematic situations in the world. Breathe love onto these situations.

4. Notice if anything changes.

Fifteen

"If the only prayer you ever say in your entire life is 'Thank you,' it will be enough."

Meister Eckhart

Being Grateful

> *Practice Fifteen: Gratitude is a positive emotion* or attitude in acknowledgment of a benefit that one has received or will receive. As a spiritual tool, it involves shifting one's focus from what one doesn't have to what one does have, no matter how seemingly insignificant.

Claudia woke up and felt the sun streaming on her face. It irritated her that she'd been awakened before the alarm went off. In a half-awake state, she rolled over and saw her journal. In a moment of inspiration, she realized, "I don't have to feel grumpy, I have choices."

She opened the journal and started writing down all the things that had changed for her in the past few months and realized she was seeing beauty in all kinds of things that she hadn't seen before.

Claudia drove to her session with Kathryn, reflecting on all the time they'd spent together. Once they were settled down, Kathryn said, "Claudia, as we agreed, this is our next to last session. Do you recall that when you began you were feeling tired and angry?"

"You know that it is almost hard to remember, but I do," Claudia said.

"Over the last few months," Kathryn continued, "you have learned different skills and attitudes that have offered you a different perspective on life. You now have choices to help you react differently. You are more aware of how you think and how your behavior affects the way you feel and most importantly you have taken on your spiritual reality and begun to find the meaning and peace inherent in it."

"Today the spiritual practice is Gratitude."

"I know," Claudia interrupted, "Why don't I list all the things for which I'm grateful?"

Kathryn laughed and said, "Right on cue, Claudia. Seriously, the quickest way to turn a lousy day around is to focus on what you are grateful for in your life - no matter how insignificant it may seem."

Claudia smiled in recognition

Kathryn continued, "The Buddha reportedly said for us to 'rise up and be thankful, for if we didn't learn a lot today, at least we learned a little. And if we didn't learn a little, at least we didn't get sick. And if we did get sick, at least we didn't die. So let us all be thankful in all things.'"

"Well, that puts things in perspective, doesn't it?" said Claudia. "OK, so, I'm really grateful that I feel so much better. I have a sense of direction, of what's important, of my place in the world. I'm grateful that for now, David's mother seems to be in a reasonably good place around her diagnosis and that I was able to hold both of them with compassion last weekend. I still have a ways to go, but I just feel hopeful and so grateful to you for helping me."

"Thank you for trusting me. I've really enjoyed our time together, and want you to know that I'm always here for you," said Kathryn.

"I'm so glad I found you," said Claudia. "My life just feels so different - in a very, very good way."

"Next week will be our last session, Claudia," Kathryn offered.

"Remind me what we agreed to talk about."

"The importance of service is the last practice in the series for developing a spiritual life. Why don't you think about what you would like to as your service activity for next week."

"I will, thanks so much, Kathryn," said Claudia as she reached out to give Kathryn a hug.

Gratitude Exercise:

Every night, write down five things for which you are grateful.

Bonus:
Take the five items for which you are grateful and imagine, individually, that they no longer exist in your life. Bring as much detail to the outcome of these losses. Then slowly, come back to the original list and notice how your gratitude deepens.

Sixteen

"No matter how busy one is, any human being can assert his personality by seizing every opportunity for spiritual activity. How? By his second job by means of personal action, on however small a scale, for the good of his fellow men. He will not have to look far for opportunities."

Albert Schweitzer

Giving Back

> **Practice Sixteen: Give back through service.**

As they settled into their seats for their last meeting Kathryn asked, "Claudia, what are you smiling about, you look so happy?"

"I am. Last week you asked me to think about what I wanted to do for service. Well it took me one nanosecond to come up with the idea of doing PR for child advocacy programs."

"That's wonderful Claudia," Kathryn said. "You talked about how fulfilled you felt in your work in public relations. Now marrying that with your commitment to children and families is a great focus for you."

"I know. I have already contacted the local advocacy group and I have an interview at the end of the week." Claudia said excitedly. "I heard it's a paid position which would help at home, while also being of service."

"Creating a balanced lifestyle that includes service to others can help you feel less stress, more connected to your spirit and more grateful for what you do have."

"Doing something like this will give my life more meaning," Claudia said. "I know I will feel better about myself because I will be giving back, doing my part."

"Yes, you will also become less invested in the rat race that is so easy to get caught up in," Kathryn said. "Many people find that that not only does service reduce stress it gives our lives a depth of satisfaction that can't be found anywhere else."

"What do you do for service, Kathryn?" asked Claudia.

"I have adopted a young man who is in a group home for the mentally ill. His parents have both passed so I have taken on the responsibility of being his guardian. I enjoy Billy and I get a great satisfaction knowing that I am making a difference in his life," Kathryn shared.

"Wow, that's great," remarked Claudia. "I guess you practice what you preach."

"I hope so Claudia." After a moment Kathryn said, "As for you, if you recall we agreed that today is our last session. When I am ending sessions with my clients I like to know what they found helpful and what is left unfinished and how they plan to work on it."

"It doesn't end here, does it Kathryn?" asked Claudia.

"No Claudia, not for any of us," Kathryn smiled. "The Journey is the Destination."

"I like that," said Claudia. "Wait, let me write that down."

When Claudia finished she looked up. "You know Kathryn, I knew today was the last session, so I looked over my journal last night. I just knew you were going to ask me what I learned."

"Well I have said that you are a great student…"

"Thanks," Claudia said and smiled. After a moment she said, "Anyway, one of the highlights for me was understanding my anger better. The practices that helped me were claiming my shadow especially when we talked about my mother-in-law. I didn't realize how much I need to not judge my anger and hold myself and others with compassion," Claudia explained.

"Yes, your anger was one of reasons you gave for seeing me," said Kathryn.

"The part I really liked though was understanding that I am a spiritual being in physical form. Once I 'got' that, everything seemed to change. My eyes were opened to the mystery in life, the synchronicity," Claudia said excitedly.

"And you saw the value in choosing 'Faith not Fear,'" Kathryn offered.

"That's basic isn't it? I am constantly asking myself: 'Fear or Faith, Claudia? You decide.'"

"Claudia, you are amazing."

"Thank you. I know that there are spiritual practices I will continue to work on, on a daily basis," Claudia said.

"Which ones stand out for you?" Kathryn asked.

"Forgiveness and living in Non-Judgment. Not necessarily forgiving others, as much as really forgiving myself. Not being so hard on me."

"Trying to love yourself the way God loves you?" Kathryn offered.

"Yes, something like that," Claudia said.

"And how is your relationship with Jeremy and David?" Kathryn asked.

"Better, definitely better. Both relationships are a work in progress. I understand that now. I'm enjoying Jeremy more and David has a couple of new job leads. I do feel more hopeful and can definitely see how I can make things better. I am more positive and I am more able to accept what is, not trying to control everything."

"Are you keeping up with your journal?"

"Yes, every day I am using my journal to write what I am grateful for. It helps to keep me centered," Claudia said.

"Oh, one more thing."

"Yes Claudia?" Kathryn said.

They both chuckled.

"I am really much more mindful. I stop myself at random times and just breathe in where I am. I always feel calmer right away. It also keeps me from racing." Claudia said.

"What can I say, except that you have been an absolute joy to work with," Kathryn said with heart.

"I am going to miss you Kathryn," Claudia said as her eyes filled with tears.

"Thank you for being willing to take this walk with me, Claudia. Please keep in touch and let me know how you are doing," Kathryn said.

"I will," promised Claudia.

Bibliography

The Authors' Favorites

A Hidden Wholeness, Parker Palmer, John Wiley & Sons, 2004, ISBN -0-7879-7100-6

A Path With Heart, Jack Kornfield, Bantam Books, 1993, ISBN 0-553-37211-4

A Return to Love, Marianne Williamson, Harper Perennial, 1992, ISBN 0-06-016374-7

Ask and It Is Given, Learning to Manifest Your Desires, Ester and Jerry Hicks, Hay House, 2004, ISBN 978-1-4019-0459-3

Boundaries of the Soul: June Singer, Anchor Books 1972, ISBN 0-385-47529-2

Callings, Finding and Following an Authentic Life, Gregg Levoy, Random House, 1998, IBSN 0-609-80370-0

Change Your Mind and Your Life Will Follow, Karen Casey, Conard Press, 2005, ISBN 1-57324-213-6

Everyday Grace: Having Hope, Finding Forgiveness, and Making Miracles, Marianne Williamson, Riverhead Books (2004), ISBN 1573223514

Goddesses in Older Women, Archetypes in Women Over 50, Jean Shinoda Bolen, Quill, 2001, ISBN 0-06-092923-5

Let Your Body Interpret Your Dreams, Eugene Gendlin, Chiron Publications, 1986, ISBN 0-933029-01-2

Meditation as Medicine: Activate the Power of Your Healing Force, Dharma Singh Khalsa and Cameron Stauth, Fireside, 2001, ISBN 0-7434-0065-8

Mutant Message Down Under, Marlo Morgan, HarperCollins 1994
ISBN 0-06-017192-8

Radical Acceptance: Embracing Your Life with the Heart of a Buddha, Tara Brach, Ph.D., Bantam Dell, 2003, ISBN 0-553-38099-0

The Dark Side of the Light Chasers, Debbie Ford, Riverhead Trade, 2010 ISBN 1594485259

The Four Agreements, Don Miguel Ruiz, Amber –Allen Publishing, 2000, ISBN 1-878424-48-3

The Miracle of Mindfulness: A Manual on Meditation, Thich Nhat Hanh, Beacon Press, 1987, ISBN 0-8070-1232-7

The Power of Now, Eckhart Tolle, Namaste Publishing, 1999, ISBN 1-57731-152-3
The Seekers Guide, Elizabeth Lesser, Villard Press 1999 ISBN 0-679-78359-8

The Wisdom of No Escape And the Path of Loving Kindness, Pema Chodron, Shambhala Classics, 2001, ISBN 0-8-7773-632-4

Transforming Anger: The HeartMath Solution for Letting Go of Rage, Frustration, and Irritation, Doc Childre and Deborah Rozman, New Harbinger Publications, 2003, ISBN 1-57224-352-X

Traveling Mercies: Some Thoughts on Faith, Anne Lamott, Anchor Books, 1999, ISBN 0-385-49609-5

Wherever You Go There You Are, Jon Kabat-Zinn, Hyperion 1994, ISBN 1-56282-769-3

Carol Solberg Moss, LCSW

Carol is a licensed clinical social worker with a Master of Social Service Degree from Bryn Mawr College in PA. She began her clinical career at the Renfrew Center in PA. In 2009, she completed spiritual direction training through the Institute for Spiritual Leadership in Chicago and is a also a certified EMDR therapist. Carol serves as adjunct faculty for Argosy College, Chicago and has given over 50 seminars and presentations on topics relating to parenting, self- care, body image and stress reduction. Carol has a private practice in Wilmette, Illinois where she lives with her family. She is also a professional singer. www.carolmoss.com

Antoinette Mercier Saunders, Ph.D.

Antoinette is a licensed clinical psychologist, who has been working with children and adults for the last 35 years. After teaching at the University of Illinois Medical School, in 1980 she founded and directed The Capable Kid Counseling Centers. Dr. Saunders has co-authored two parenting books, *The Stress-Proof Child* and *Focus on Children*. In addition to writing numerous parenting columns and articles, she has appeared on more than 400 TV and radio shows, here and in Great Britain. In 1988 Dr. Saunders trained in spiritual direction at the Institute for Spiritual Companionship. She is presently founder and co-director of Transformations: the Institute for Psychological and Spiritual Development, (www.spiritualtransformations.org)

Transformations co-sponsors the annual Women's Spirituality Conference in Northfield, IL every winter. Dr. Saunders is also in private practice and lives in Wilmette, IL with her family. www.antoinettesaunders.com

LaVergne, TN USA
13 February 2011
216357LV00002B/2/P